30 Burnham Beeches

39 Boulder; August 1977

44 Hug Baby Blues

57

62

64

28 Living In The Moment

26 you burn in my cup of oil and I glow

Also by Marilyn Hacker

PRESENTATION PIECE
SEPARATIONS

TAKING
NOTICE

TAKING NOTICE

MARILYN HACKER

ALFRED A. KNOPF   NEW YORK   1980

THIS IS A BORZOI BOOK
PUBLISHED BY ALFRED A. KNOPF, INC.

Copyright © 1976, 1978, 1979, 1980
by Marilyn Hacker

Library of Congress Cataloging in Publication Data
Hacker, Marilyn [date]
    Taking notice.
    I. Title.
PS3558.A28T3   811.'54   79–28166
ISBN 0–394–51223–5
ISBN 0–394–73917–5 pbk.

Manufactured in the United States of America
First Edition

Acknowledgment is gratefully given to the following magazines, in which some of the poems in this book originally appeared: *Ambit, American Rag, Bananas, Calyx, Conditions, Confrontation, Frontiers, The Little Magazine, Missouri Review, Ms., The Nation, Open Places, Ploughshares, Salmagundi, Shenandoah, A Shout in the Street, Sinister Wisdom*, and *Woman Poet*.

"Adult Entertainment" originally appeared in *Partisan Review*.

"Burnham Beeches," "The Hang-Glider's Daughter," "Lines Declining a Transatlantic Dinner Invitation," "A Man With Sons," and "Third Snowfall" originally appeared in *Poetry*.

"Introductory Lines" was composed for the Formal Poetry issue of *The Little Magazine*, vol. 11, no. 3.

"Iva's Pantoum" originally appeared in *Chrysalis* (Los Angeles), no. 6, pp. 44–45.

"Moon Animation" and "Shirland Road" are reprinted by permission from *New England Review*, vol. 2, no. 4 (Spring 1980).

"Pantoum" originally appeared in *13th Moon*.

"Partial Analysis" originally appeared in *Christopher Street*.

"Prayer for My Daughter" originally appeared in *Millennial Women*, edited by Virginia Kidd, published by Delacorte, 1978.

"The Regent's Park Sonnets" originally appeared in *The American Poetry Review*.

"Taking Notice" was originally published as a chapbook by Out and Out Books, New York, 1980.

The fourth line of "La Fontaine de Vaucluse" is paraphrased from H. D.'s *Tribute to Freud*, published by McGraw-Hill, 1974.

for Marie Ponsot, Bill Brodecky, and Cynthia Macdonald

The author wishes to thank the MacDowell Colony and the Foundation Karolyi for providing the time and space in which much of this book was written.

CONTENTS

FEELING AND FORM

Feeling and Form   3

LIVING IN THE MOMENT

Sequence   9
The Regent's Park Sonnets   14
Little Green-Eyed Suite   19
Part of a Letter   24
Sonnet   26
Rondeau After a Transatlantic
    Telephone Call   27
Living in the Moment   28
Burnham Beeches   30
Adult Entertainment   31
A Man With Sons   32

THE HANG-GLIDER'S DAUGHTER

To Iva, Two-and-a-Half   37
Prayer for My Daughter   38
Boulder: August 1977   39
Three Sonnets for Iva   40
Up From D.C.   42
Huge Baby Blues   44

Third Snowfall   46
Iva's Pantoum   48
The Hang-Glider's Daughter   52

OCCASIONS

Sonnet Ending With a Film Subtitle   57
Introductory Lines   58
For Getting Started in a New Place   60
Lines Declining a Transatlantic
    Dinner Invitation   62
Iva's Birthday Poem   64
July 19, 1979   66
Partial Analysis   67
Tranche Romancière   68

LA FONTAINE DE VAUCLUSE

Conte   73
Why We Are Going Back to
    Paradise Island   74
Visiting Chaldon Down   76
Ordinary Women I   79
Ordinary Women II   80
Shirland Road   83
La Fontaine de Vaucluse   84
Peterborough   88
Moon Animation   91
August Acrostic   92
How It Happens   93

Home, and I've   94
Five Meals   96
Pantoum   98
From Provence   102
Canzone   104

TAKING NOTICE

Taking Notice   109

FEELING AND FORM

FEELING AND FORM
for Sandy Moore and for Susanne K. Langer

Dear San: Everybody doesn't write poetry.
A lot of people doodle profiles, write
something they think approximates poetry
because nobody taught them to read poetry.
Rhyming or trailing gerunds, clumps of words
straggle a page, unjustified—poetry?
It's not like talking, so it must be poetry.
Before they learn to write, all children draw
pictures grown-ups teach them how not to draw.
Anyone learns/unlearns the craft of poetry
too. The fourth grader who gets a neat like-
ness of Mom in crayon's not unlike

the woman who sent you her Tone Poem, who'd like
her admiration praised. That isn't poetry,
unless she did the work that makes it like
this, any, work, in outrage, love, or lik-
ing an apple's October texture. Write
about anything—I wish I could. It's like
the still-lives you love: you don't have to like
apples to like Cezanne. I do like words,
which is why I make things out of words
and listen to their hints, resounding like
skipping-stones radiating circles, drawing context from text, the way I've watched you draw

a pepper shaker on a table, draw
it again, once more, until it isn't like
anything but your idea of a drawing, like an idea of movement, drawing its shape from sequence. You write poetry.
I was a clever child who liked to draw,
and did it well, but when I watch you draw,
you rubber-face like I do when I write:
chewed lip, cat-tongue, smiles, scowls that go with right
choices, perplexed, deliberate, withdrawn
in worked play, conscious of the spaces words
or lines make as you make them, without words

for instant exegesis. Molding words
around a shape's analogous to drawing these coffee-cups in settings words
describe, but whose significance leaves words
unsaid, because it's drawn, because it's like
not my blue mug, but inked lines. Chosen words
—I couldn't write *your white mug*—collect words
they're meant, or drawn to, make mental space poetry
extends beyond the page. If you thought poetry
were merely nicely ordered private words
for two eyes only, why would you say, "Write
me a letter, dammit!" This is a letter, right?

Wrong. Form intimates fiction. I could write
me as a mathematician, weave in words
implying *you* a man, sixteen, a right-
handed abstract expressionist. I'd write
untruths, from which some other *you* could draw
odd inferences. Though I don't, I write
you, and you're the Donor on the right-
hand panel, kneeling in sable kirtle. Like-
ly I'm the lady left of you, who'd like
to peer into your missal, where the writing (legible Gothic) lauds in Latin poetry
the Lady at the center. Call her poetry,

virtual space, or Bona Dea. Poetry
dovetails contradictions. If I write
a private *you* a public discourse, words
tempered and stroked will draw you where you draw
these lines, and yours, convergent, made, unlike;

that likelihood draws words I write to poetry.

LIVING IN THE MOMENT

SEQUENCE

1

A woman is talking to you. You represent
only yourself, usual, unique:
a man half listening to a woman speak
words also about words. You are absent;
you are silent. If I tried to fake
disinterested reason, I would fail.
I've smoked so much my mouth is rank and stale.
I've drunk enough to be just half awake.
If you walked in I wouldn't know what to do.
Damn them and their freedom, said my friend,
her lover off to Greece, Chip teaching child-
free seminars, you, your car piled
with books, approaching Penzance or Ostend,
and beside you, a woman is talking to you.

2

Rocks, heather, mud, veered up from either side
of the thin road like a crease between hills.
Stout ponies munched the scrub. We were chilled
through with the fine rain, even inside
your heavy car, but I gasped with a child's
joy at the breadth and height of that wild place.
The car's broad jaw crunched branch. Your clenched
    face
gripped the road, when it was clear, you smiled
at the road if not at me, peopled the crags
with relatives and friends, and then with loss
of which you didn't speak. Rain splats, talk sags.
I watched you and the hills, twice alien.
Needles of light ravelled the clouds. A cross-
post pointed us back to London again.

3

Beautiful to me, you have lived in it long
enough to think, I think, any song
in your body's praise puerile. You never loved yourself
much, howevermuch I love your face
when your mouth cracks free from gloom, unexpected
    grace
across a room, at an overfilled bookshelf.
I'd like to make you words as physical
as waking with hungry skin, an extravagant
shudder to touch, like a branchy plant
palming the window with bright leaves. Beautiful,
but who wants one, these starved days being rational
and rationed out? You are very real
when I dream you into bed; you feel
for the misplaced key, and drive off, as usual.

4

Across unmeasured distances between
proximities, you find me anyway
easily. What comes over me, the way
I come over you? Well enough left alone,
but I'm not. Once I could celebrate
the darkness we collided in; how much
more difficult to parse some sense to touching a friend in daylight. Recapitulate:
tragedians accept the Status Quo
as a Good Thing, try to alter it and go
to the waiting dogs, however nobly. We
will not be tragic heroes, love, okay?
I think the status quo has had its day.
Revolutions feed on comedy.

5

Solemn, unfunny, earnest, doctrinaire,
I grip you in a four-hour verbal wrangle
as we postpone another sort of tangle.
We smoke. I twist my legs around the chair-
legs (hoping that they will wind
later with yours), light up from butts. We drink.
Do I bother to find out what you think?
You'll say that you can't say what's on your mind
(or don't I ask till we're too drunk to care?)
Towards morning, in the wordless dark upstairs
our hands and mouths continue discourse, guide
us sometimes to a meeting. While the birds
wake up, we sleep. Naked, I lie beside
you, naked, with a head still full of words.

6

What good are words if none of them can free
us from our imagined selves? You are
one man, not some indifferent Muse to me.
(We women poets have no stock of far-
fetched icons to keep you suitably far
from our aggrandized passions.) Can we see
beyond the ineffectual crass car-
icatures the mirror limns when we
have learned from lovers, analysts and B
movies we aren't what we ought to be?
Guilt, loneliness, self-pity, jealousy,
bound from the words I tweak for poetry,
and hung back, graceless, words that say we are
not free, but more free than we'd like to be.

7

But this, five days ago a baby died
should not have died, healthy, loved, cared-
for by her one mother, too prepared
for loss by loss. I am blank inside
as the child loses her name. No one will say:
Lucy Aviva Scott, in her twelfth week,
died in her crib. Too cowardly to speak,
I write, and my gut convulses while I play
with my loud live child. But this: how can I be
free, with a spoilt obscenity of choice,
reasonably whole, reasonably sane,
if I cannot look at the torn pain and the numb pain
lived in, not out; only with a hushed voice
blank out the dead child too sharp to see?

8

My bat-eared baby sleeping bottom up,
your three sons with their mother's copper hair,
hold us to our wished selves, hostage to their
futures. There the resemblance stops,
at a rift between memory and change.
I don't trust the lost past you'd like to save;
my brave alternatives you'd call a Brave
New World, raw and discomforting and strange.
I called her Lucy because when we were
in Sweden, there was a kind of midwinter
queen, called Lucy. There was a feast for her
on the shortest day, to give you hope. That's why
she was Lucy, for light on a dark day.
Choice is a gift. Choice is a luxury.

THE REGENT'S PARK SONNETS

1

"That was in another country," but the wench
is not yet dead, parks the red-striped pushchair
near the Rose Garden and turns loose her fair
Black Jewish Woman Baby; picks a bench
scoured by warm winds; (five years ago, twelve days
and nights, another country, where the might-
be was incarnated every night),
squints, focussing on the child, not yours, who plays
explorers. You are in another count-
ry, house-guesting, annual August rounds
as solid as ripe apples, on the grounds
of continuity, convenience (*Con!*
suggests itself; it seems I can't be hon-
est and not too bitter or too blunt).

2

You rang me up this morning from Marseilles
echoing other lines and other lives.
The best-intentioned women sound like wives
sometimes: why couldn't I find something to say
but "When will you be back?" Above the playground, like a capsuled world, a plane
heads, fortunately, north. Fresh after rain
the sky is innocently blue. Away
from frisking kids, including mine, I write
stretched on a handkerchief of pungent dry
grass, wishing I could take off my shirt.
I word old wounds. As usual, they hurt
less. Iva's giving someone's bike a try.
We could be on a plane tomorrow night.

3

Some table-talk at lunch, of memory:
the anecdotal hypnotist who could
unlock the nursery. Not babyhood
occurred to me, but two weeks buried by
the next five years. That's when I should have made
poems each extraordinary day
and I could read them now and brush away
the dust accrued over a half-decade,
and I'd remember everything we said
when I thought we were saying everything.
We did, I guess, what everybody does,
if I were better at remembering.
Sometimes I wonder who I thought I was
and who on earth I thought was in my bed.

4

"What's in a park they warn girls out of?" "Queers."
That's what I thought of parks at seventeen:
hunting-grounds, pleasure-gardens, never seen
by day eyes, girls' eyes, blinkered eyes like theirs—
the clucking mums on benches near the swings.
I've joined their number after fifteen years.
I'm sure behind the bushes after hours
all sorts of lewd and fascinating things
still happen. But they won't happen to me.
If I were tall and tan and twenty-three,
I still would be a woman. So I stay
among women and children, on the day
side, guarding a blue pail and red spade.
I wonder how they manage to get laid?

5

One master, aged, as I am, thirty-two,
all summer sonneted adulterous
love: cocktails and woods, fortuitous
meetings, public words that no one knew
were private. This playground is an odd landscape for longings in an afternoon
splashed with babies' bright clothes. Near six
    now. Soon,
grown tired of high adventure in the sand-
pit, we will head for home and food.
We—you and I—don't have a thing to hide.
We need not meet through pseudonyms and gin.
Yet there's no common space for meeting in,
and secrets fence me in on every side.
This week is taking longer than it should.

6

Another poet, woman and alive,
recalls: sorrow is politics. Another
woman, not my tormentor, not my mother,
waits for you, in a castle. Gosh! We thrive,
it seems, on *Woman's Own*. On women's own
solitude, uncertainty, old fears
nursed, like a taste for brandy, over years.
"If you don't mind, I'd still rather not know
you." Wound like clockwork, she and I,
speechless, oppose. Central, you stroke one, strike
the other. In New York, I lived with two
men; we loved each other. Do you *like*
either? Replaceable, we know it, sigh,
resigned, while options preen in front of you.

7

Thursday, the eighth of August, four o'clock.
Fire-salvaged wood desk filled the window bay,
notebook, cat curled round coleus: the way
I spent those afternoons. Downstairs, a knock.
Midnight at the Savoy-Tivoli
still talking; me guilty you paid the bill
while I was in the john. Bar, home, alone, still
dazed. Paul and Bill: "Have you noticed he's
most attractive?" "Oh, shut up!" Ninety-one
degrees today, in London. On the dock
flushed kids queue for canoes. Iva, in bright
blue shorts, clambers the bench. On Friday night
hands brushed in the dark, stayed: finished, begun.
—Friday, the eighth of August, four o'clock.

8

Gino's hummed an epithalamion:
one resident fag-hag and paedophile
reformed! You knocked *Jack Daniel's* back in style.
In two days you would go and fetch your son.
Meanwhile bought rounds. I think groped Nemi's knee.
I almost minded. Under the table, gripped
my legs in yours. "Let's go." My cronies quipped
farewells. (The pub downstairs, less leisurely,
disgorges footsteps and unsteady songs
bracketed by cars.) Late through the long
night, our tongues grappled in a double cave.
Naked swimmers plunged in wave over wave,
hands, mouths, loins, filling and filled, until we gave
ourselves back, tired, seawashed and salty, strong.

(Coda)

It was not my mother or my daughter
who did me in. Women have been betrayed
by history, which ignores us, which we made
like anyone, with work and words, slaughter
and silver. "The Celts treated their women well . . ."
(I guess their wives were Picts.) A man at a table—
like you, whose face is etched on my nights, unable
to see as I see that first face first in hell-
ish uncertainties, and then unlearn, relearn.
The peach-faced Cypriot boy brings us more wine.
Cryptic, perhaps, yes, as this hedged return.
I choke up, as if I had breathed water.
Other, not polar, not my mother or daughter.
Some woman might have understood the line.

LITTLE GREEN-EYED SUITE

"... this way of grief
is shared, unnecessary
and political"
   Adrienne Rich: "Translations"

1
November, Saturday night:
outside, raining,
inside, the electric fire,
Gauloises and big black ashtray, coffee,
the carpet clean—first time in years.
Yvonne just left, to feed her cats
before going back to Max's.
Bill is exploring the city.
His watercolors
are up, two bright rows
above my worktable,
and Judith's linocut
and Peter Reinstorff's poster
—me swathed in plastic and a gasmask—
finally framed and hung.
"Timid, vibrating unspoken needs,"
that's, perhaps, me
and you,
relieved when I left,
"looped now in the liana of her arms,"
(courtesy of Frank O'Hara).
Hammers in my head, guts hot cement,
half the night in the rue Dauphine

my thoughts wheeled back
to knocking her downstairs, smashing
her face in! Not
yours, of course, not yours.
Later, dreamed
of coming back to find
wreckers at my house,
the stairway gone,
walls painted black,
and letters from you that had lain in the rain.

2
Maybe tonight she's gone home to do her laundry,
gone home to write her copy,
gone home to meet a woman
friend, to tell about her new
life, muddles she's rescued you
from. Maybe tonight you're
with old friends from the country,
cooking leek and potato
soup just for the children
and you, reading old letters
(mine), going upstairs alone
to bed, maybe recalling
us in bed together
(if there was any difference),
maybe just glad to be
alone. She'll be back
tomorrow, last night she was
there, but
(I tell myself at midnight,
or two, switching the light off)
not, maybe, tonight.

3
How dare the brass-
assed bitch jackboot
and magpie into your life
with a camouflage of potted plants
hurling a passing payload
of self-igniting shit on invisible me?
But if some brass-bottomed
bastard bombed into my bed and board,
would I mind? Oust him on your account?
Salvage my solitude? Now, no.
Before? Was it
misery I was sworn to,
not you, for years of near-fidelity?

4
I eat a thick soup of pain,
sleep with pain,
wake up swollen and sore
as a flaming jaw of impacted teeth.
Anger's the only pill
but it wears off in an hour or a day
and, slapped brat, I whimper, Why not me?
Why wasn't I whatever I'd have to be
to share an ordinary
life, as she suddenly and easily
does, eating and sleeping and waking
with you, coming back every day from a day
in the world? I fudge a hurt
guess, stir sludge on a page

you won't see. Leave me alone to mend,
heal, harden. You never were my friend.
I don't know what we were. Don't pretend
you really somehow thought I wouldn't mind;
remind me that you're there just to remind
me when you have nothing to say
but "Sorry." Yes, sorry. Now go away.

5
Back, gloomy, to the Hayward Gallery, a
winter Sunday with Bill. Nudging September, we
circled chryselephantine sculpture,
stroked a sphinx, onyx and ivory.
Bronze monkeys blew Tiffany-glass bubbles.
You were just back from holidays in France.
I was five months with Chip's and my baby.
We didn't say what we wanted with each other.
Rodin hulks evolved upstairs;
Gaudier-Brzeska turned
curious plane on plane to the light;
fin de siècle wax dissolved flesh to tears.
These Burne-Jones women are your relatives
whose fine bones colonize Wales and Stockwell,
your lady in print velvet dressing gown.
Herself beguiled, Nimue, wrenched from her book,
stares through grey-locked Merlin's stunned eye-blaze.
The monkeys bat their precious bauble spheres
in a smart gallery, rue Saint-Denis.

6

"Is it any improvement," said Chip
(in the Hungarian restaurant),
"to go from a man who's gay
to one who wishes he were?"
I wish I were a Lesbian.
(I pepper the lentil soup.)
"Honey," says Bill,
"if you could take a *pill*
to be a Lesbian, you'd
walk on down the street and home
in on Ms. Wrong before you got to the post office!"

PART OF A LETTER

Poems I wrote you in Tourrettes
are in anthologies.
I've given up French cigarettes.
I stand and watch the trees

silver-boled and sprocketed
with infant April green,
fists of jonquils pocketed
in dry branch in between,

blown and jostled up the slope
soundless beyond the case-
ment's seal. My bus was late. She hoped
after I'd washed my face

—here was my room—and had a rest,
I'd join them downstairs. "We've
a cocktail party for the guest
poets in forty-five

minutes." Square beige rugs—twenty feet—
two beds, desk, mirrors, view,
five lamps, a quiet source of heat,
a bathroom tiled dark blue,

outdo Amsterdam Avenue,
certainly Marylebone.
Thousands of miles away from you,
all this past week I've gone

from bus to bus to common room
of questioning scrubbed faces:
Why do you have this running theme
of exile? In what places

do you write best? Do poets earn
a living? How? Where can
I publish? Can a woman learn
writing from a man?

Dusk, and I henscratch this to you
which, after you have seen
it, may meet more public view
in some small magazine,

which doesn't make the distance hurt
less, or me less tender—
both senses. Now, in a clean shirt,
to drinks with Mr. Spender.

Matte brandy bottle, adjacent voices, skin
of flank, hip, and ribs trade warmth. You stroke
me, stroke into me. We come together,
come, come back, front on front, where we were.
Ordinary lamplit lovers, we smoke
and whisper. You burn in my cup of oil
and I glow. Our voices flicker, still
alight. As it happens, this never happened.
We sat, traffic-jammed in the rented car
after hours piled up. We were tentative.
You would go again. A barred signal, "love"
hung between us where we stalled. Desire
tautens parallel perpendiculars;
a thin wire lights and shadows where I live.

RONDEAU AFTER A TRANSATLANTIC TELEPHONE CALL

Love, it was good to talk to you tonight.
You lather me like summer though. I light
up, sip smoke. Insistent through walls comes
the downstairs neighbor's double-bass. It thrums
like toothache. I will shower away the sweat,

smoke, summer, sound. Slick, soapy, dripping wet,
I scrub the sharp edge off my appetite.
I want: crisp toast, cold wine prickling my gums,
love. It was good

imagining around your voice, you, late-
awake there. (It isn't midnight yet
here.) This last glass washes down the crumbs.
I wish that I could lie down in your arms
and, turned toward sleep there (later), say, "Goodnight,
love. It was good."

LIVING IN THE MOMENT

"This is a seasick way,
this almost/never touching, this
drawing-off, this to-and-fro."
   Adrienne Rich: "The Demon Lover"

Two blue glasses of neat
whiskey, epoxy-mended Japanese
ashtray accruing Marlboro and Gauloise
butts, umber and Prussian blue ceramic cups
of Zabar's French Roast, cooling. You acquired
a paunch; I am almost skinny
as I'd like to be. You are probably
right, leaving. We've been here
thousands of miles away, hundreds of times before.

I try to be a woman I could love.
I am probably wrong, asking
you to stay. Blue cotton jersey
turtleneck, navy corduroy Levi's,
nylon briefs, boy's undershirt, socks, hiking shoes:
inside (bagged opals, red silk swaddles a
Swiss Army knife) a body nobody sees.
Outside, cars and men screech on Amsterdam Avenue
hundreds of times, before, thousands of miles away,

hidden in cropped hair like a lampshade,
I try to say what I think I mean.
My thirty-five-year-old white skin wants you
to stroke back twenty-seven-year-old certainty
I'd better doubt. The time-stopped

light hours ago on the smelly East River
glazes my eyes with numbers, years. We both
wear glasses. We both have children
thousands of miles away. Hundreds of times before,

we agree, the nerves' text tricked us
to bad translation. My wrapped sex cups
strong drink. A woman honed words
for this at an oak desk above the Hudson
River in November; cross-legged on woven straw
in a white room in a stucco house; locked
in the bathroom away from the babies, notebook
on her knees. I repeat what we were asking
hundreds of times before. Thousands of miles away,

I am leaving you at Heathrow. Revolution
of a dozen engines drowns parting
words, ways: "I should be asking you to stay."
I shouldn't be asking you to stay. We finish
our courage. Tumblers click on the table.
Tumblers click in the lock. I unwrap
cotton and corduroy, nylon and cotton,
wrap up in flannel for the night that started
thousands of miles before, hundreds of times away.

BURNHAM BEECHES

At two A.M., chain-smoking in your car,
I unironically must praise you for
choosing an overdue fidelity
to someone who has got no use for me.

We might have used each other if we could.
Lost at late twilight in an ancient wood,
we are not changed much on Midsummer's Eve.
We spiral miles to find the car and leave.

Inhabited or not, the present trees
incorporate us in mythologies;
we think they do as they bulk out in ours
—I should say "I" and "mine." Indifferent powers,

boled Bona Dea, Druid patriarch,
nor mock nor bless in the forestalled half-dark.
I flesh them with what separates us: sex,
as we sit on a log, just out of reach

of each other's reminiscent hands.
Rain slants the last light through sibilant branches.
We scuff out cigarette butts on the ground,
turn up our collars and retrieve the road.

I hope we shared the manna of the place.
I choose to praise your necessary choice
that nothing was engendered in the wood
but powers that would have changed us if they could.

ADULT ENTERTAINMENT

Agreed: Familiarity breeds
confusion; cautious consistency is better.
You would be harried; I (and she) be hurt.
Sane speaking distance is safest and best.

Under an academic tweed
jacket, over a second-hand Shetland sweater,
a cotton jersey and an undershirt,
your naked hand welcomes my naked breast.

A MAN WITH SONS

for David Batterham

You come back with a heaped shopping basket:
a huge romaine, a wholemeal loaf, tomatoes.
You put a big chipped saucepan on to boil,
dip the tomatoes on a ladle. "What
are you doing to them, Dad?"
The eighteen-year-old looks up from his letter.
"Taking off their skins." Nonfunctional,
I straddle a wooden chair, watch
you sieve the scalded, peeled pulp-globes
into (you tell us) last night's fish broth.
My friend's just made her way here from the Tube,
climbs from the lower room, contentedly
ungloving book-dust from her elbows, adds
cadenza to the kitchen colloquy.
My stomach calms an octave into speech.
Stained mugs, newspapers straggle off the table
as the boys straggle in. One, fourteen
looking ten, overalled, leaves
a postcard album on a cluttered shelf.
Svelte in T-shirt as your bronze Florentine
namesake, the questioning middle one makes room
for his leather-jacketed, apricot-cheeked friend
who lives here too. The twenty-year-old
painter, slicked back damp from summer job
lifeguarding, eye-sockets blackberry blotches:
"I got in a fight. Really, I got fought on.
Who wants," he slices, back to us, "some bread?"
Now there is a salad on the table,
green, orange, purple, frilling a wooden bowl.
You plunk down odd plates, ceramic porringers

your brother made. If an ailanthus tree
strained through the splintery floorboards,
     it would be me,
leaf-pores dilated toward you, perhaps because
this is complete without me. Pouring water, you pose
inadvertently, with the two younger boys
bent toward your chair. The big window behind
the table frames you with a bricked-in garden
where a transplanted pet's five-fingered leaves
stretch to the light. My friend, mother of sons,
pours warm baritone laughter on the banter
like burgundy. Milk, water, Coca-Cola
gurgle in glasses. She roots me
(boy-lover once, once your lover, a daughter's
mother) to the other plot I garden
weeding out nostalgia. Your soup is good
as your boys' voices, bread shared on a board
(as little or as much as we can share).
I weigh the paradox of praising you
for what, unpraised, daily, most women do,
a praise, a paradox I can't afford.
You heap my plate with salad, wedge of bread,
after my friend's, before your youngest's; then
the grown boys amicably seize the bowl.
Made adversaries by tired ironies
at midnight, failures of nerve, failures of charity,
bad actors in humiliating roles:
primeval woman, archetypal man,
who clutch, abandon, claim, betray, demand;
friends in noon's grace we are forgiven, whole.

THE HANG-GLIDER'S
DAUGHTER

TO IVA, TWO-AND-A-HALF

Little fat baby, as we
don't run the world, I
wince that I can't
drive a car or a truck, ice-
skate, build shelves and
tables, ride
you up five flights of
stairs on my shoulders.
I notice you noticing
who rides most of the Big
Motorcycles, drives buses,
stacks grocery cartons, makes
loud big holes in the street.
"Mustn't hit little girls!" meaning
you, though who'd
know if we didn't say so!
Soon they'll be telling you
you can't be
Batman, Shakespeare, President, or God.
Little fat baby, going on
schoolgirl, you can be
anyone, but it won't be
easy.

PRAYER FOR MY DAUGHTER

You'll be
coming home alone on the AA
Local from Canal St., 1 A.M.
Two black girls, sixteen, bushy
in plaid wool jackets, fiddle
with a huge transistor radio.
A stout bespectacled white woman reads
Novy Mir
poking at a grey braid.
A thin blue blonde dozes on shopping bags.
Tobacco-colored, hatchet-faced and square,
another mumbles in her leather collar.
Three sharp Latinas jive round the center-post,
     bouncing
a pig-tailed baby, tiny sparkling
earrings, tiny work overalls.
A scrubbed corduroy girl wearing a slide-rule eyes
a Broadway redhead wearing green fingernails.
A huge-breasted drunk, vines
splayed on cheeks, inventively
slangs the bored brown
woman in a cop suit, strolling.
You'll get out at 81st St. (Planetarium)
and lope upstairs, travelling light-years.
The war is over!

BOULDER: AUGUST 1977

Curves converge and blossom in your face;
leaf-shapes ripple a patterned snake
safe through pied grass. A tacky diamondback
linoleum, earth, russet, green, and black,
covers my rented table. Typescript heaps
await parenthesis between our sleeps.
You're asleep now, murmuring, in the other room.
The mountain range has a domestic name;
I am domesticated at its foot,
flabby, diasporid, illiterate
in lichens, grasses, insects, conifers.
Here is a white man lettering AFRICA
on a scrapbook of Tarzan movie stills.
Reading it is my work. A woman whirls
her nightgowned daughter on her hip. Night gowns
them, whirls them, us, through different windows,
    down.

THREE SONNETS FOR IVA

He tips his boy baby's hands in an icy
stream from the mountaintop. The velvet cheek
of sky is like a child's in a backpack
carrier. Then wrote his anthology
piece, began it while she changed the Pamper
full of mustardy shit. Again rage
blisters my wet forehead as the page
stays blank, and you tug my jeans knee, whimper
"I *want* you!" I want you, too. In the child-
sized rowboat in Regent's Park, sick with a man,
and I hadn't spoken to another
grown-up for two days, I played Amazon
Queen and Princess with you. You splashed pond water
outside my fantasy, nineteen months old.

The bathroom tiles are very pink and new.
Out the window, a sixty-foot willow
tree forks, droops. Planted eighteen years ago,
its huge roots choke the drains. The very blue
sky is impenetrable. I hear you
whine outside the locked door. You're going to cry.
If I open the door, I'll slap you. I've
hit you six times this morning. I threw
you on the rug and smacked your bottom. Slapped
your face. Slapped your hands. I sit on the floor.
We're both scared. I picked you up, held you, lov-
ing your cheek's curve. Yelled, shook you. I want to stop
this day. I cringe on the warm pink tiles of
a strange house. We cry on both sides of the door.

Chip took you to your grandmother's today.
You scoop sand-cakes from your orange-and-blue
dump truck, while he reads *The Times Book Review*
on a hot slatted bench four feet away.
Solitary for work, I pay bills, spray
the roaches' climbing party on the flank
of students' dittoed manuscripts and bank
statements. Myself as four-year-old, I play
with your clean clothes, open my closet, finger
old lives' skirts dependent on plastic hangers.
You ask for dresses now, and I demur,
then buy you a crisp shift, blue with white cats,
which I just once have offered you to wear.
I love you most when you are what I'm not.

UP FROM D.C.

We were six women. My lover
was the youngest. Her cabled shoulders
glistened like her short dark hair.
Tucked, unnoticed, in a sprawling slum
our house was under siege.

We were six women, one
my lover, in a wooden
house, waiting
for the danger
to be over.

In a round tin tub
a woman scrubs
the shape from a baby's
face. The plump brown
child's red hair-ribbon tells: a girl.
Immerses her again, head
under. I cry out, seize her.
You, baby-shaped, face
shapeless, sprawl in a
deck chair. I run, gasping, grab
you too. Is it too late?
Your chins lump like putty.

We looked out a cracked window
on the second floor, from a bare
room: scorched floorplanks, cobwebs.
Dust. Dusty outside,
porched row houses of a Southern slum,
one, cater-corner across, enamelled red.

Coffee cans sprout grapefruit shrubs from pits.
An old black woman in a faded print
dress sits behind them, rocking,
waiting for the danger to be over.

Her sweaty runner's limbs
sprawl across mine, arm on
my shoulder, calf
knotted against my knee. We hunch
below the windowsill, cramped. Still
heat. Roaches run errands.
Her angular
cheekbones glint like blades.
After this, we will not
scavenge. We hope
to survive. The others move
lightly in the hallway. One bald bulb
dangles. One of them
may have given us away.

I try to run with the two
limp puckered babies
grasping my neck, still
chilly and damp, my arms
under their buttocks, their plump
legs slack. Is it too late?

Light squeezes through bamboo slats.
I squeeze my eyes shut. Corduroy
wales pleat my skin through sheets.
You're awake, humming, in the other room,
golden and rosy, blue Grow Pajamas
over scabby knees. In a minute
we will lock on the day's love, the day's rage.
In a minute I will hold you in my arms.

HUGE BABY BLUES

Written with the letters that can be used in an eight-segment wiring diagram, to print out poem, letter by letter on L E D display board: A, B, C, E, F, G, H, I, J, L, N, O, P, S, U, Y.

S O S HUGE BABY LOOSE!
SHE'S FULL OF POISON APPLE JUICE,
SHE'S FULL OF PUNS 'N' LION PISS,
AS NOSY AS CHINESE POLICE.

SHE SAILS ABALONE SHELLS.
SHE SLOPS EGGS IN SCALLION SAUCE.
SHE JOINS GANGS OF YELLING PEOPLE.
SHE SLEEPS IN A USEFUL BUS.

SHE SIPS GIN ON GYPSY SHIPS.
SHE CAN CUSS IN JAPANESE:
"BABOON-BELLY-JELLO-BALLS!"
SHE SAYS SEALS CAN SING THESE SONGS.

SHE'LL HANG BACON ON PIGS' NOSES.
SHE PLAYS BALL ON FALLING HILLS.
SHE CAN LEAP IN OCEAN POOLS.
SHE CAN LAY ON SUCH A FUSS!

NINE HISPANIC FLYING NUNS
CHOOSE LUNCHES IN A GAY CAFE:
"CHOP SUEY, BAGELS, FISH SOUFFLE,
PAPAYA JUICE, PINEAPPLE FLAN,

SOY SAUCE, YES, OH, COFFEE, PLEASE
I FANCY A BANANA ICE."
SHE CAN PINCH A BUSY CHEF
COY AS ANY CABIN BOY.

LUNCHES, GLASSES, SLIP, FLOP, BANG,
SPILLING, SPLASHING, SLIPPING, GLOP!
A BASHFUL CHEF HAS BOILING BUNS.
FLYING NUNS FLAP, FLY, ESCAPE!

HAIL FALLS ON A SLUSHY PLAIN.
SHE IS LONELY AS A SLUGGISH
SPANIEL PUPPY IN A PIGPEN.
NO ONE SINGS A SONG IN ENGLISH.

NO ONE SINGS A SONG IN SPANISH.
SHE IS YOUNG AS JANIS JOPLIN'S
CHOICE OF BESSIE'S EPIC BLUES.
SINGING NUNS CAN BE SO CLANNISH.

SUN IS SHINING, FINE AS FOIL,
ON AN OCEAN BILGY BLUE.
OUCH! I FEEL A FISH AS FLIPPY
AS A FELON FLEEING JAIL

BICYCLING ON SOGGY SPINACH
FEEBLY LEGGY AS A FOAL.
CALL A CAB IN HALF AN—NO
I'LL PENSION OFF A CHANCY FINISH,

COUGH UP AN ESOPHAGUS
FULL OF GOLDEN ONION SOUP . . .
SHE'S A BILIOUS GENIUS, YES.
IF SHE'S NOISY, SHE'S LESS FUSSY.

SHE IS HIGHLY FALLIBLE.
CAN SHE SPELL? OH NO! A BANG!
GUNS OF GIGGLING JELLY BEANS?
BABBLING ANGELS GO INSANE.

THIRD SNOWFALL

"Take with you also my curly-headed four-year-old child."
Josephine Miles: "Ten Dreamers in a Motel"

Another storm, another blizzard
soaks the shanks and chills the gizzard.
Indoors, volumed to try a Stoic, a
four-year-old plays the *Eroica*
three times through. Young Ludwig's ears?
No, only an engineer's
delight in Running the Machine.
Pop! Silence? "I was just seein'
if I could make the tape run back."
"Don't." "If the knob is on 8-track
and I put on a record, what
happens? . . . It's turning, but it's not
playing." "That's what happens." "Oh.
Which dial is for the radio?
I'm going to jump up on your back!
Swing me around!" A subtle *crack*
and not-so-subtle knives-in-spine.
"Get down, my back's gone out! Don't whine

about it, I'm the one that's hurt."
"I'm sorry . . . Did I have dessert?
What's water made of? Can it melt?"
(I know how Clytemnestra felt.)
"I want a cookie. What is Greek?
Will I be taller by next week?
Is this the way a vampire growls?
I'm going to dress up in the towels.
Look! I can slide on them like skis!
Hey, I've got dried glue on my knees.
Hey, where are people from? The *first*
ones, I mean. What was the Worst
Thing you Ever Ate?" *Past* eight
at last, I see. "Iva, it's late."
"It's not. I want some jam on bread."
"One slice, then get your ass in bed."
"No, wait until my record's over.
I want my doll. And the Land Rover
for Adventure People. Mom, are
you *listening*? Where's the doll's pajamas?
There's glue or something in my hair.
Can I sleep in my underwear?
I think I need the toy fire-fighter
guy too . . . I'm thirsty . . ." *und so weiter.*

IVA'S PANTOUM

We pace each other for a long time.
I packed my anger with the beef jerky.
You are the baby on the mountain. I am
in a cold stream where I led you.

I packed my anger with the beef jerky.
You are the woman sticking her tongue out
in a cold stream where I led you.
You are the woman with spring water palms.

You are the woman sticking her tongue out.
I am the woman who matches sounds.
You are the woman with spring water palms.
I am the woman who copies.

You are the woman who matches sounds.
You are the woman who makes up words.
You are the woman who copies
her cupped palm with her fist in clay.

I am the woman who makes up words.
You are the woman who shapes
a drinking bowl with her fist in clay.
I am the woman with rocks in her pockets.

I am the woman who shapes.
I was a baby who knew names.
You are the child with rocks in her pockets.
You are the girl in a plaid dress.

You are the woman who knows names.
You are the baby who could fly.
You are the girl in a plaid dress
upside-down on the monkey bars.

You are the baby who could fly
over the moon from a swinging perch
upside-down on the monkey bars.
You are the baby who eats meat.

Over the moon from a swinging perch
the feathery goblin calls her sister.
You are the baby who eats meat
the bitch wolf hunts and chews for you.

The feathery goblin calls her sister:
"You are braver than your mother.
The bitch wolf hunts and chews for you.
What are you whining about now?"

You are braver than your mother
and I am not a timid woman:
what are you whining about now?
My palms itch with slick anger,

and I'm not a timid woman.
You are the woman I can't mention;
my palms itch with slick anger.
You are the heiress of scraped knees.

You are the woman I can't mention
to a woman I want to love.
You are the heiress of scraped knees:
scrub them in mountain water.

To a woman, I want to love
women you could turn into,
scrub them in mountain water,
stroke their astonishing faces.

Women you could turn into
the scare mask of Bad Mother
stroke their astonishing faces
in the silver-scratched sink mirror.

The scare mask of Bad Mother
crumbles to chunked, pinched clay,
sinks in the silver-scratched mirror.
You are the Little Robber Girl, who

crumbles the clay chunks, pinches
her friend, gives her a sharp knife.
You are the Little Robber Girl, who
was any witch's youngest daughter.

Our friend gives you a sharp knife,
shows how the useful blades open.
Was any witch's youngest daughter
golden and bold as you? You run and

show how the useful blades open.
You are the baby on the mountain. I am
golden and bold as you. You run and
we pace each other for a long time.

THE HANG-GLIDER'S DAUGHTER
for Catherine Logan

My forty-year-old father learned to fly.
Bat-winged, with a magic marble fear
keeping his toast down, he walks off a sheer
shaved cliff into the morning. On Sunday
mornings he comes for us. Liane and I
feed the baby and Mario, wash up, clear
the kitchen mess. Maman is never there;
that is the morning she and Joseph try
to tell the other pickers how the Word
can save them. Liane gets me good and mad
changing her outfit sixteen times, while I
have to change the baby. All the way
up the hill road she practices on him, flirt-
ing like she does at school. My back teeth hurt

from chewing Pepper Gum on the bad side.
She's three years younger. I'm three years behind.
Did he *mean* that? Shift the gum. Did I remind
Mario, if the baby cries, he needs
burping? I can stretch out on the back seat.
The olive terraces stacked in the sunshine
are shallow stairs a giant child could climb.
My hiking shoes look giant on my feet.
Maman says "a missed boy." What do I miss?
I wonder what the word in English is
for that. Funny, that we should have been born
somewhere we wouldn't even understand
the language now. I was already three
when we left. If someone hypnotized me

would I talk English like a three-year-old?
The bright road twists up; bumpily we shift
gears, breathe deep. In the front pouch of my sweat-
shirt, I've still got my two best marbles. Rolled
in thumb and finger, they click, points gained, told
beads. Not for Joseph's church. If I forgot
French, too, who would I be inside my head?
My hands remember better: how to hold
my penknife to strip branches, where to crack
eggs on a bowl rim, how to pile a block
tower—when I was little—high as my nose.
Could I, still? The box of blocks is Mario's
now. My knee's cramped. I wish that I could walk
to Dad's house, or that I was up front, talk-

ing to him. How does he feel, suddenly slung
from brilliant nylon, levering onto air
currents like a thinking hawk? I'd be scared.
I'd be so scared I can't think it. Maybe a long
slope on my skateboard's like that. Climbing
isn't scary: no time. The air's fizzy, you're careful what rock you hang your weight from, and where
your toes wedge. My calves ache, after, ribs sting,
but I'm good for something. What I like high
is mountains. I'll go up the hill behind
Dad's house this afternoon. I'll pick Liane
flowers. Nahh, we'll be leafing magazines
for school clothes on the sun porch after lunch.
I like those purple bell-spikes. My cleats crunch

the crumble; I stretch to the ledge and pull
out the whole rooted stalk. Sometimes there's twelve
bells, purple as—purple as nothing else
except a flower, ugly and beautiful
at once. Across my face come the two smells:

53

grandmother's linen-chest spice-sweet petals
and wet dirt clinging, half meat, half metal,
all raw. Between them I smell myself,
sweaty from climbing, but it's a woman's
sweat. I had one of the moon dreams again.
I stood on the flyover facing purple
sea, head up, while a house-huge full moon hurtled
toward me; then it was me flying, feet still
on the road. We're here, on top of the hill.

OCCASIONS

SONNET ENDING WITH A FILM SUBTITLE

for Judith Landry

Life has its nauseating ironies:
The good die young, as often has been shown;
Chaste spouses catch Venereal Disease;
And feminists sit by the telephone.
Last night was rather bleak, tonight is starker.
I may stare at the wall till half-past-one.
My friends are all convinced Dorothy Parker
Lives, but is not well, in Marylebone.
I wish that I could imitate my betters
And fortify my rhetoric with guns.
Some day we women all will break our fetters
And raise our daughters to be Lesbians.
(I wonder if the bastard kept my letters?)
Here follow untranslatable French puns.

INTRODUCTORY LINES

Rushing to press, it still would seem evasion
not to compose a Verse for this Occasion
to introduce and celebrate our choices
of forms shaped by contemporary voices
(received forms, or invented, or adapted
from Norse, or Anglo-Saxon as one chap did).
At best form gives concinnity, precision,
paring of words and widening of vision,
play for the mind, focus that is self-critical.
Poets, and poems, are not apolitical.
Women and other radicals who choose
venerable vessels for subversive use
affirm what Sophomore Survey often fails
to note: God and Anonymous are not white males.
"We always crafted language just as they did.
We have the use, and we reclaim the credit."

One form perennially apposite,
the useful garment of the sonnet fit
lover, fabulist, feminist, and wit
—those categories not, of course, exclusive.
Concise, ornate, colloquial, allusive
language tidewashed Cathedral Station's floor,
low pun to philosophic metaphor.
A camera on a rotating boom,
six words spin slowly round and pan the room:
I would not like to have to choose between a
sestina on composing a sestina
and one that's a whodunit thirty-nine

lines long—and science fiction has a fine
champion, in sonnet sequence. Bible and fairy,
sexy, perverse, domestic, cautionary
tales are told, some controversy sowed.
There's one syllabic, one Pindaric ode.
There's birth, love, death, work, solitude (no money,
oddly enough). There's quite a lot that's funny,
and everything that's funny is not slight.
Poets who always, poets who seldom write
in forms, well-known or unknown, all responded.
(*Please* don't send whole verse novels, like someone
    did!)
A Wiccean muse, Form can transform like Circe.

P.S.   There are no haiku; that's a mercy.

FOR GETTING STARTED IN A NEW PLACE

Invoke the pines, the bushy oak,
the young girl's bed in which you woke
hugging an absent body; call
on: coffee in the dining hall,
three black cups, slice of brown-bran toast,
the Jewish woman fabulist
of gruesome verisimilitudes,
the chunky plates of breakfast foods
for the matutinal colonists.
Invoke your daughter, whom you kissed
and tickled, yelled at, sang to, stroked,
put on a yellow bus; invoke
your mother at cantankerous
senile sixty-eight; her nurse
whose Caribbean histories
people the close Bronx room as she
bridges archipelagoes.
Invoke whatever you can use;
sebaceous pores, querulous gut,
nostalgic genitalia, but
put them to work and shelve your self-
abusive tendencies, a shelf

already stocked with "necessary"
errands that can fill up every
minute you're not asleep, shitting,
or eating. Call on the last unwitting
prophet in Central Park playground.
Call on your mother's bank-account.
Reinflict some remembered pain;
invoke the sun out *(please!)*, the rain
away; invoke your appetite
for lunch; pick up a pen and write.

LINES DECLINING A TRANSATLANTIC DINNER INVITATION
for Charlie and Tom

Regretfully, I proffer my excuses.
Number not less than Graces, more than Muses:
Auden's casting call for a dinner party.
He was a genius who was often smart. He
did not think hosts should count their guests in pairs,
unless they had loveseats and no hard chairs.
He was benignly daft for Small Odd Numbers:
a table choked with elbows soon encumbers
wit. I'm sure you'll all be very witty.
I'll miss it, snowed in here in New York City.
But, being *d'un certain age*, we come to know:
better to be discussed than be *de trop*.
The unexpected often is disaster.
If one arrives a month or an hour faster
than looked for, something that one cannot like
might happen: cab drivers would be on strike;
one's friends would be that morning reconciled
with lover, spouse, or adolescent child,
whose tears, A-Levels, or Social Disease
will call them home before the fruit and cheese;
the woman-poet-hating editor
looms ominously near the kitchen door
where a zinc bucket slops up the cold rain
that's sluiced down since the roof fell in again;
one host is wrapped in blankets in the attic: a
damp-inspired episode of his sciatica;
the other, peeling sprouts in a clogged sink,
scowls through a fourth compensatory drink;

somebody else has brought along a new
chum who was scathing in *The New Review;*
there'd be the flight to Amsterdam at nine;
simply, there might be insufficient wine.
As passports take two weeks to put in shape,
this all may have a flavor of sour grape.
Speaking of grapes—I hope you bought *Biscuit*—
pour one more brandy, as it were, on me.

IVA'S BIRTHDAY POEM

All horns should honk like anything!
All taxicabs should come alive
and stand on their back wheels and sing
that Iva Alyxander's five!

The fish are burbling in the lake,
the bees are buzzing in their hive,
the candles flicker on the cake
that Iva Alyxander's five!

She's put on inches, weight, and speed.
Who knows what wonders may arrive.
I prophesy she'll learn to read,
now Iva Alyxander's five.

Dolphins leap in the swimming pool
to watch her famous cartwheel dive.
Jump! Flip! Swirl! Splash! *Extremely* cool,
now Iva Alyxander's five.

She'll hire a plane—she has a plan—
and teach her mother how to drive.
She can, if anybody can,
now Iva Alyxander's five.

She's smart, she's tough, you've got to hand her
that—so praise in prose and verse
the newly five-year-old Commander
(In Training) of the Whole Universe.

The Acrobats, the Metropoli-
tan Opera and the Royal Ballet
will jointly stage a birthday gala,
for you-know-who is five today!

Wonder Woman and Superman
and Robot Warriors from Mars
all pick up rainbow spray-paint cans
and write her name on subway cars.

They hand out ice cream in the station
with chocolate bars as big as bricks.
There won't be such a celebration
till Iva Alyxander's Six!

We'll toast her health! So pour a drink of
champagne, or chocolate soda! I've
the greatest daughter I can think of
and Iva Alyxander's FIVE ! ! ! ! !

JULY 19, 1979

I'll write a sonnet just to get in form,
allowing fifteen minutes by the clock
to build gratuitously block by block
of quatrains. Almost six, pale sunlight, warm
(last night we thought there'd be a thunderstorm).
The crickets fiddle buzz-saws without vowels.
I've had thrice-daily bouts of runny bowels,
which seems, on travels south, to be the norm.
I must avoid the self-indulgent stance
of lovesick troubadours—that isn't wise,
in spite of being in the South of France
with a capricious woman whose blue eyes
invest the genre with some relevance.
She says they're green. I've done my exercise.

PARTIAL ANALYSIS
(OF THE "GIUDIZIO UNIVERSALE" OF GIOVANNI DI PAOLO)
for Richard Howard

Do you imagine, wakeful late in bed,
a Gay Bar Paradiso, inlaid gold,
or are you inexplicably impelled
to Hell, where naked people eat boiled toad?

Beneath six trees in fruit with golden apples,
two boys are stroked by a greybeard schoolmaster.
A Carmelite comes up behind her sister
(praying) and smooths her cowl and cups her nipples.

A monk is taking off another monk's
belt. Two svelte blonde maidens, looking rapt,
caress each other's breasts. Pink incorrupt-
ible chubby martyred Innocents give thanks.

A nun, an Arab, and a bearded priest
exchange a blessing that goes round three ways.
Three angels have three monks down on their knees.
A cardinal greets a youth with a slim waist

cinctured in red. In Hell, it's very dark
and pasty-looking people with no clothes
are pinched and pushed and boiled in noxious baths
—it's not unlike some places in New York—

while everyone looks put-upon or bored.
But everyone looks Interestingly Bad
in Heaven, their reward for being good:
Hesperidean light, and no holds barred.

TRANCHE ROMANCIÈRE

"Franchement, je m'en fiche de la vertu!"
said Maud, letting her supple haunches sink
into the velvet armchair. "I can count
on the fingers of a defective hand
women with firm ideas on how to act
who behave themselves, by *my* standards, well!"

"No good dripping like a bucket from the Well
of Loneliness, as if there were intrinsic virtue
in taste or distaste for a harmless act.
They'll plumb the depths of gloom that they can sink
to, all unconscious, on the other hand,
of things they do for which they are account-

able." "You're such a moralist!" the Countess said. "If I didn't know you so well,
I never would imagine you could hand-
le ambiguities so brusquely. Virtue
is not, speaking abstractly, like that sink-
ing in melted chocolate feeling. Act

your age. Or mine. My great-grand-aunt the act-
ress was forgiven for her bank-account.
She started with her elbows in the sink.
Not that she did it, but that she did it well
is where you or I would locate the virtue."
She weighed a green fig in her cool cupped hand.

When she was twenty-five she had been hand-
some; thirty years in the field of action (as she called it) had had the virtue
(Maud thought) of refinement, count-
ing times her tall friend had been all-too-well
acclaimed. She spoke, making her voice sink

to philosophic alto. "We must synch-
ronize words to images. I hand
the palm to cinéastes; they make a well-
fleshed metaphor." "That kind of act
exceeds the act of kind." "Dear, I can count
on your wit; sobriety's *not* your virtue."

"I've other virtues." Standing near the sink,
the Countess pulled five rings off her right hand.
"Actually, I don't feel entirely well . . ."

LA FONTAINE DE VAUCLUSE

CONTE
(Cinderella, sometime after the affair of the glass/fur slipper)

First of all, I'm bored. It's not
what you'd think. Every day, meetings
I can't attend. I sit and sit and stick
my fingers with petit-point needles. Ladies
ignore me, or tell me all their petty secrets
(petty because *they* can't attend meetings)
about this man or that. Even his mistress
—*you* would have assumed he had a mistress—
gritted her teeth and had me come to lunch
and whined about the way she was mistreated.
And I suppose she's right, she was mistreated.
The plumbing is appalling, but I won't
go into that. He is forever brooding
on lost choices he might have made; before
three days had passed, I'd heard, midnight to dawn,
about the solitary life he craved.
Why not throw it all up, live on the coast
and fish, no, no, impossible with wives!
Why *not* throw it all up, live on the coast,
or cut my hair, teach (what?) little girls
and live at home with you? I schooled myself
for this, despised *you* for going to meetings,
reading instead of scrubbing, getting fat
(scorn of someone who burns off bread and puddings).
I made enduring tedium my virtue.
I'll have to keep my virtue. I could envy
you, but I'm sick of envy. Please allow
me now, at least, to call you sisters. Yours, C.

WHY WE ARE GOING BACK TO PARADISE ISLAND

He has just cornered and skewered
a rat with a broomstick. He once shot
a milk doe, sloppily and badly.
He let his cousin's kitten starve, to show him.
Stalking at dawn in March, when he was twelve,
he shot his small brother by mistake.

He mourns his son dead twelve hours old,
his father gulping in an oxygen
tent, the brother whose surprised
gasp explodes his waking lips again.
He hunts them down in dreams. His fat smart
baby daughter wanders in front of a truck

so he buys an identical pickup truck
and picks up another older little daughter
aged, say, eight, and drives her out to the woods
behind the motel, and bashes her when she screams.
Does he, really? He imagines
the wind, the smell of mouldy birch leaves

and blown smoke. What if he really hated
his wife, if she were nothing but a cunt
and her cunt were a swamp lined with razor-blades?
He has two wives, really. One lives on pills.
He pays her therapist. The other has
her ribs taped where he got her with a two-by-four.

Numinous and glowing, stained-glass windows,
poems crafted and spare as winter birch,
he imagines the rapist, the voyeur,
the child-murderer, the telephonist
whispering threats in the night. He imagines
hiring someone to do it to his wife

while she screams and pisses herself. No, while
she groans with delight. She takes it in her
mouth, glistening black, twice as big as his.
Would a sheep's hole feel the same, or the cold
tight gap of a beached dog-shark, last gasps
coming together, before limp flesh?

He was not the enemy. He was the hurt
idealist, poet, he read the books
you did. His manners were better than mine.
You wanted him to praise you and make you real.
I wanted to hear about his childhood.
We wanted him to love us.

VISITING CHALDON DOWN

for Jeanne Wordsworth

We left the Volvo in a cleft of grave-
barrows. The road ran out, ran down
to tractor- and pony-gouged mud. Green hills
slid from lip to cup-bowl. The heat-
meniscus lidded and lensed us, swallowed
our sounds. Not March except for harsh
plant smells; then, beyond hills, the raw sea.
Two men, two women: they, thirty years friends;
we, recent strangers. My sometime lover
in a patched tweed jacket, heard, probably
not for the first time, your sometime husband
(vast glasses and a pea jacket, peppered
hair over the collar) juxtapose
Romans on Powys and his brace of Yankee
wives. One had Chidioch farmhouse, one
the garden shed. You thrust wide fists down
in sandy cardigan pockets, scuffed
mud, worried by the irrational
like a big pup's leather bone. You muffled
your angles in orphan clothes. Six years younger than
everyone, Levi's, green corduroy,
I faked bold, not even on approval.
I wanted to wander away, clamber the hills
as usual, wanting (as usual)
to incise his hand on me (it wasn't)
with bright air, mint wind, on chalk

cliff-face with the dead poets, already told
to gorse and cowshit, huddled scrub and stones.
What stones did you grasp and shy
in your own head, on approval in the narrow
smoky kitchen with the lodger's wooden ladder
guiding her platform wedgies down, your own
two daughters, plumpish and pasty, shy
of your shying some unanswerable
through antemenarchal calm? My own
daughter was across the ocean we climbed to.
What can a woman say to another woman,
almost a stranger, toeholding through
an invisible war? I said almost
nothing, held back and held your hand
when your sandal skidded.
                                    Dear Jeanne, believe
under all probable beliefs this is
for you. Edna Millay, foreign as I, once walked
across the Downs to cheer that sick man, wrote
one of the stories, without the women. I
read it today: Chaldon Down, Bat's Head; thought
of you. In a bony cove, bottle-green
threaded gravel a white drop down. I sprawled
between two men, on a pebbled spit
jutting sheer lucidity, shying
pebbles, with you wedged in my mind,
reasonably terrified, landlocked behind
us in the muddy pasture.
                                    (Reasonably
terrified in the prison of unreason-
able women, you turn and turn a matchbox

over, label-side, wooden-side, on your palm:
the pictured purple flame is numinous;
what is its name?)
                    Over fried eggs
congealing toward thick white-bread toast, across
formica, steam from mugs of weak tea,
I asked if it hurt. We need words
for pain's phyla: cracked ribs, the murderess' next
moment, the birth-work, death snapping
the fan of possibilities
shut, the mind seeded or winged
with uninvited energies. "Sometimes
it fills me with force and joy. The terror
is where it will leave me." Misremembered,
your ripe voice is hybrid. You
were foreign too.

ORDINARY WOMEN I

I am the woman you see in Blooming-
dale's ruffling the rack of children's sweaters
on sale, trying on tweed slacks in Better
Sportswear, which I won't buy, browsing and homing
in on unmatched striped sheets on January
Clearance. Rapt with textures, women escalate
leisurely. This is our protectorate.
Our brown or pink skins flush over furry
or frayed coats in smoothing taupe light. We do
not shuffle aside for the man, who is
not here, who built this shelter, our consuming
career. What I am saying to you is
I am the woman you will see blooming
up from our terror, with women: me, you.

ORDINARY WOMEN II
for June Jordan and Sara Miles

Mrs. Velez of the Tenants' Association
zig-zags her top-heavy shopping cart through
the usual palette of dogshit, brick-red
to black on grimy leftover snow.
Tenement roofs' stone scrollwork
soot-chiaroscuro on the almost-equinoctial
sky. Old Mrs. Cohen, who still wears a marriage wig,
stiff-legs the stoop with Food City-bagged garbage.
Slashed bags everywhere spill chicken bones,
orange peels, crushed milk cartons, piss-soaked
Pampers, broken toys.
Sweat-cracked loafers, runover orange work shoes,
    silver-painted
platform shoes, running-stripe sneakers, a cast on one
    foot
and newspaper-stuffed single shoe, electric-blue-
    patent-leather-
style-fake-yellow-snakeskin-trim shoes, stand,
pace,
shuffle,
Bop a little,
in front of the liquor store; the hands man brown-
    bagged Ripple.
She has a daughter named Tequila,
little and black and wiry and so is she,
her name's Joanne.
Yellow-trousered Tequila, rising three,
dashes from the separator to the laundry scales,

past two broken dryers.
Sometimes she plays with Iva on the slide.
"I'm OK, I'm goin' to night school, studying
bookkeeping,
but I gotta leave Tequila with my brother—
that's him."
He must be nine,
little and black and wiry, leafs
Spiderman, The Incredible Hulk beside him
on the bracketed row of plastic chairs.
Tequila's run outside.
"Joseph, go *get* her!" He does.
Joanne has a textbook, *American History*,
all-sized thumb-smudges on the library
binding. She has me write my name and number
on a creased notebook-leaf shoved inside.
"What you doin', Tequila? Stay by me, you hear!"
I feel my old brown sheepskin's London label,
my red wool ERA cap . . . Joseph herds
Tequila toward the thrumming washing-
machines. She
scooters a canvas basket to the porthole.
Her left blue Flintstones sneaker is untied.
Tile walls sweat steam and soap. Compact Anne
     Desirée,
the proprietaire, has my laundry folded
into the Macy's shopping bag. "Comment ça va?"
"Très bien, merci." "Et ta fille?" "Grandissante,
a l'école au moment. Merci bien, au revoir. Bye,
Joanne, Joseph, Tequila!"
Threadbare brown corduroy coat, Army Surplus
     safari jacket,
orphaned suit coat, raddled blue anorak, black leather
     bomber jacket,

pastel polyester plaid with calf-length back-
    split skirts,
elbow outside the liquor store;
the hands man brown-bagged Ripple.
The woman who stands on street corners stands
on the street corner, her coffee-bean
skin ashy, her plump face Thorazine
swollen. Thin grey coat gaps open
on short white housedress gapped open
on bolstered brown knock knees.
Fragile flesh puffs sink her huge wet eyes,
not looking across the street, or down the street,
not looking at the sidewalk or the sky.

SHIRLAND ROAD

for Yvonne

This is the other story. There are three
women in a room. Fat glasses, tea-
pot not cleared away, we draw up tides
of talk that clear the beaches and subside
to amicable silence; sip, smoke, lean
back into notebooks, newspapers. The green
unfabled garden darkens. One of the cats
thumps in the window, rumbles on a mat-
ted cushion near the red bars of the fire.
Beyond the magic circle of desire
where shadows stall in storied attitudes,
this continues happening. Warmed blood
unclenches toes and fingers, which can stroke
cat, cushion, massed black hair tangled with smoke
and rosewater. You have strewn second-hand
treasures on all your surfaces, that find,
question, dismiss the eye; buff, blue, brown things
I like. Have we been quiet for a long
time? Vermouth, Eleanor of Aquitaine.
A red moth skitters on the windowpane.
Brown flowers glow on globed light above strewn
books.
Marie is writing, too. You've gone to cook
supper: brown garlic, slice a cucumber.
I track my nose into the kitchen, stir
up salad dressing, filch a corner of cheese,
teetering on a balance bridging these
planks of resignation and repose.

LA FONTAINE DE VAUCLUSE

for Marie Ponsot

"Why write unless you praise the sacred places . . . ?"
    Richard Howard: "Audiences"

1

Azure striation swirls beyond the stones
flung in by French papas and German boys.
The radio-guide emits trilingual noise.
"Always 'two ladies alone'; we were not alone."
Source, cunt, umbilicus, resilient blue
springs where the sheer gorge spreads wooded,
    mossed thighs:
unsounded female depth in a child-sized
pool boys throw rocks at. Hobbled in platform shoes,
girls stare from the edge. We came for the day
on a hot bus from Avignon. A Swed-
ish child hurls a chalk boulder; a tall girl,
his sister, twelve, tanned, crouches to finger shell-
whorls bedded in rock-moss. We find our way
here when we can; we take away what we need.

2
Here, when we can, we take away what we need:
stones, jars of herb-leaves, scrap-patch workbags
    stored
in the haphazard rooms we can afford.
Marie and I are lucky: we can feed
our children and ourselves on what we earn.
One left the man who beat her, left hostages
two daughters; one weighs her life to her wages,
finds both wanting and, bought out, stays put, scorn-
ful of herself for not deserving more.
The concierge at Le Régent is forty-six;
there fifteen years, widowed for one, behind
counters a dun perpetual presence, fixed
in sallow non-age till Marie talked to her.
I learn she is coeval with my friends.

3
I learn she is coeval with my friends:
the novelist of seventy who gives
us tea and cakes; the sister with whom she lives
a dialogue; the old Hungarian
countess' potter daughter, British, dyke,
bravely espoused in a medieval hill
town in Provence; Jane whom I probably will
never know and would probably never like;
Liliane the weaver; Liliane's daughter
the weaver; Liliane's housewifely other
daughter, mothering; the great-grandmother
who drove us through gnarled lanes at Avignon;
the virgin at the source with wedgies on;
Iva, who will want to know what I brought her.

4

Iva, who will want to know what I brought her
(from Selfridge's, a double-decker bus,
a taxi, Lego; a dark blue flowered dress
from Uniprix; a wickerwork doll's chair
from the Vence market; books; a wrapped-yarn deer;
a batik: girl guitarist who composes
sea creatures, one of three I chose,
two by the pupil, one by the woman who taught her),
might plunge her arms to the elbows, might shy stones,
might stay shy. I'll see her in ten days.
Sometimes she still swims at my center; sometimes
she is a four-year-old an ocean away
and I am on vertiginous terrain
where I am nobody's mother and nobody's daughter.

5

"Where I am, nobody's mother and nobody's daughter
can find me," words of a woman in pain
or self-blame, obsessed with an absent or present man,
blindfolded, crossing two swords, her back to the water.
The truth is, I wake up with lust and loss
and only half believe in something better;
the truth is that I still write twelve-page letters
and blame my acne and my flabby ass
that I am thirty-five and celibate.
Women are lustful and fickle and all alike,
say the hand-laid flower-pressed sheets at the
        papermill.
I pay attention to what lies they tell
us here, but at the flowered lip, hesitate,
one of the tamed girls stopped at the edge to look.

6

One of the tamed girls stopped at the edge to look
at her self in the water, genital self that stains
and stinks, that is synonymous with drains,
wounds, pettiness, stupidity, rebuke.
The pool creates itself, cleansed, puissant, deep
as magma, maker, genetrix. Marie
and I, each with a notebook on her knee,
begin to write, homage the source calls up
or force we find here. There is another source
consecrate in the pool we perch above:
our own intelligent accord that brings
us to the lucid power of the spring
to work at re-inventing work and love.
We may be learning how to tell the truth.

7

We may be learning how to tell the truth.
Distracted by a cinematic sky,
Paris below two dozen shades of grey,
in borrowed rooms we couldn't afford, we both
work over words till we can tell ourselves
what we saw. I get up at eight, go down
to buy fresh croissants, put a saucepan on
and brew first shared coffee. The water solves
itself, salves us. Sideways, hugging the bank,
two stocky women helped each other, drank
from leathery cupped palms. We make our own
descent downstream, getting our shoes wet, care-
fully hoist cold handsful from a crevice where
azure striation swirls beyond the stones.

PETERBOROUGH

Another story still: a porch with trees
—maple and oak, sharpening younger shoots
against the screen; privileged solitude
with early sunlight pouring in a thin
wash on flat leaves like milk on a child's chin.
Light shifts and dulls. I want to love a woman
with my radical skin, reactionary im-
agination. My body is cored with hunger;
my mind is gnarled in oily knots of anger
that push back words: inelegant defeat
of female aspiration. First we're taught
men's love is what we cannot do without;
obliged to do without precisely that:
too fat, too smart, too loud, too shy, too old.
Unloved and underpaid, tonight untold
women will click our failings off, each bead
inflating to a bathysphere, our need
encapsulated in a metal skin,
which we, subaqueous monsters, cannot in-
filtrate. The middle of the road is noon.
Reactive creature with inconstant moon-
tides (no doubt amendable as near-
sightedness, but sacred to How Things Are)
my blood came down and I swarmed up a tree,
intoxicated with maturity.
Woman? Well, maybe—but I was a Grown-
Up, entitled to make up my own

mind, manners, morals, myths—menses small price
to pay for midnight and my own advice.
By next September, something was revenged
on me. Muffled in sweat-soaked wool, I lunged
out of seventh-grade science lab, just quick
enough to get to the Girls' Room and be sick.
Blotched cheeks sucked to my teeth, intestines turning themselves out, hunched over a churn-
ing womb fisting itself, not quite thirteen,
my green age turned me regularly green.
Our Jewish man G.P. to whom I carried
myself hinted sex helped, once you were married.
Those weren't days I fancied getting laid.
Feet pillowed up, belly on heating pad,
head lolled toward Russian novel on the floor,
I served my time each hour of the four
days of the week of the month for the next ten
years, during which I fucked a dozen men,
not therapeutically, and just as well.
Married to boot, each month still hurt like hell.
The sky thickens, seeps rain. I retrospective-
ly add my annals to our tribe's collective
Book of Passage Rites, and do not say
a woman gave notebook leaves to me today
whose argument was what I knew: desire,
and all the old excuses ranked, conspired:
avoid, misunderstand, procrastinate;
say you're monogamous, or celibate,
sex is too messy, better to be friends
(thirsty for draughts of amity beyond
this hesitation, which has less to do
with her than my quixotic body's too

pertinacious—*tua tam pertinax*
valetudo, neither forward nor back-
ward—malingering, I ask, or healing).
I like her: smart, strong, sane, companionate.
I still love a man: true, but irrelevant.
Then, unavoidably, why not?
She was gone (of course) by this time; I sat
mirrored, eye-to-eye, cornered between
two scalp-high windows framing persistent rain.

MOON ANIMATION

Someone left the keys in that bronze antique
two-seater. The border's not unthinkably far.
We've been sleeping together for a week.
Nothing is impossible anymore.

On the wooded road, our two lean shadows stretch
morning-long in a triple-bill spectacular
moonrise. You tell tall tales of the bowling witch.
Nothing is impossible anymore.

Graveyard moonlight, insufficiently grave
to ground me. I may just swim twenty-four
laps tomorrow. In your lap's one nice place.
Nothing is impossible anymore.

Big as an incandescent volleyball,
the swelled globe drifts to zenith. I explore
your cheek, neck, shoulder, anything at all.
Nothing is impossible anymore.

With shuddering strokes, we offer the full moon
to each other. My hand sinks to the wet core
of your heat and our nerves fugue on a twinned tune.
Nothing is impossible anymore.

AUGUST ACROSTIC

Sunshine is pouring me full of moonshine.
Apolitical twinges shiver through
Nascent blackberry-ripenings, while I
Drowse in an extremely overgrown
Yard. I roll in long grass

Muttering to my fool self iambic
Oracular limericks. Your various
Orifices intoxicate, surfaces likewise.
Reeling between liquefaction and
Evaporation, I teeter on the taste all day.

HOW IT HAPPENS

Really, it's a coeducational
boarding school. The big girls complain about
the boys: spotty, spoken-for. They do without
those gymnastic recreational
pastimes, compensate in the dining hall
with Scrabble and lime fizz. One gawky sweet
long-limbed math whiz and one dour Semit-
ic Latin grind are keeping their council
on the topic, trudge in the woods in the rain
instead, get giddy at intramural
events, slope off, slanting, before the bell.
Doors wedged shut in a pink-wallpapered room
they prime their adolescent epicene
genius on specialized curriculum.

HOME, AND I'VE

Covered the flowered linen
where I graze
on a convolvulus that hides in
lion grass, and ride in-

to the sunrise on a sand
horse. These days
shorten, but the afternoon simmered
me down. I had dinner

alone, with retrospective
on the blaz-
on of your throat's tiger-lily flush
and your salt sap enough

company until tomorrow.
The fat blue
lamp spills on a ziggurat of books,
mug the same cobalt. Looks

like reprise of lesson one
in how to
keep on keeping on. Easier, with
you fixed hours away; both

solitude and company
have a new
savor: yours. Sweet woman, I'll woman-
fully word a nomen-

clature for what we're doing
when we come
to; come to each other with our eyes,
ears, arms, minds, everything wide

open. Your tonic augments
my humdrum
incantations till they work. I can
stop envying the man

whose berth's the lap where I'd like
to roll home
tonight. I've got May's new book for bed,
steak, greens, and wine inside

me, you back tomorrow, some
words, some laz-
y time (prune the plants, hear Mozart) to
indulge in missing you.

FIVE MEALS

"A table means does it not my dear it means a whole steadiness"
  Gertrude Stein: *Tender Buttons*

Slices of ham, pâté, sausage, on lettuce leaves;
cauliflower, wedge of duck in a browned wine
sauce; lettuce, raw cabbage, vinegar and oil;
a square of walnut cake with mocha frosting;
Camembert in green foil, a hard roll, butter;
a half-bottle of champagne, black coffee.

Croissants, butter, orange juice, coffee.
Beaujolais versus St. Emilion. Bibb leaves
with grated sheep's cheese; snails in garlic butter;
roast suckling pig crackling in juice; red wine
in a glass pitcher; chocolate mousse. Breath frosting
the glass in your hand. Brandy in bed. Oil

cost a lot, in huge bottles. Without oil
we ate endive, goat cheese. No coffee
take-outs in Paris. The crème fraîche, peaked like
      frosting,
you scooped up with moon-green feather-shaped leaves
cross-legged on the bed. We uncorked wine
with my Swiss knife. Between sour cream and butter:

I lick fingers of cream. The gold-foiled butter
cube you've shaped, between jam labels, in oil
crayons. Tongues are smoothed by rough young red
     wine.
The drawing's edge is a brown stream of coffee.
You save one tangerine with two long leaves
curling the globe. Dark chocolate, like torte frosting

out of the bowl. Morning, cold rain frosting
the cubed panes. Croissants, tartines and butter.
We're still sleepy, but neither of us leaves
a crust. I stroke your peach-furred cheek; hot oil
wells from the source as the first milky coffee
pours down. You have no crayons for the wine

colors. We could only drink white wine
but it's too cold. The rain puddles are frosting
over. We plan excursions with more coffee.
You fold the currant jelly and the butter
labels. In Florence there'll be olive oil
cheap, in baroque tins. Our train leaves

at seven. I leave our New Year's wine
frosting in the kitchen. Rainbows of oil
swirl on warm smells: buttered fresh bread, strong
     coffee.

PANTOUM

There is a serviceable wooden dory
rocking gently at the lip of ocean,
from where her moorline loops back loosely
to an outrider of the wet forest.

Rocking gently at the lip of ocean,
whorled and rosy carapaces glimmer.
To an outrider of the wet forest
who kneels at the undulant flat belly

whorled and rosy carapaces glimmer
under, the water is a mirror dreaming.
Who kneels at the undulant flat belly
feels her pulse gyre in the liquid circles.

Under the water is a mirror dreaming
furled leaves. She kneads and presses her friend's spine,
feels her pulse gyre in the liquid circles
her palm oils on smooth skin, opening like

furled leaves. She kneads and presses her friend's spine,
enters her own blood's tiderush, leaves
her palm oils on smooth skin. Opening like
shrubbery parting to bare fingers, she

enters. Her own blood's tiderush leaves
her charged with flammable air, igniting the
shrubbery. Parting to bare fingers, she
grows, reaches into the fire licking

her, charged with flammable air, igniting the
dry tinder, and the wet places that flame like brandy.
Grows, reaches into the fire licking
her clean, that nourishes as it consumes

dry tinder. And the wet places that flame like brandy
are knowledgeable. They affirm
her: clean. That nourishes as it consumes
detritus of self-doubt, whispers she fears

are knowledgeable. They affirm
each other in themelves. Still, when the
detritus of self-doubt whispers, she fears
the empty pool, that secret. They could lose

each other in themselves, still. When the
postcards begin arriving, they depict
the empty pool, that secret. They could lose
jobs, balance, money, central words, music.

Postcards begin arriving. They depict
themselves living in a perfect landscape, with
jobs, balance, money: central. Words, music
one made for the other, late at night, as they rocked

themselves. Living in a perfect landscape, with
passionate friends, you'd ache, she thinks.
One made for the other? Late at night, as they rocked
into incognate languages, were they still

passionate friends? You'd ache, she thinks,
if your mind buzzed with translations of denial
into incognate languages. Were they still
anywhere near the hidden rainforest?

If your mind buzzed with translations of denial,
you might not see the gapping in the hedgerows,
anywhere near the hidden rainforest,
a child could push through, or a tall woman stooping.

You might not see the gapping in the hedgerows
at first. She grew up here, points out where
a child could push through, or a tall woman. Stooping,
howevermany shoulder in, to the brambles

at first. She grew up here, points out where
the path mounts, damp under eye-high ferns.
However many shoulder into the brambles,
each one inhales the solitude of climbing.

The path mounts, damp under eye-high ferns.
Cedars aspire to vanishing point in the sky.
Each one inhales the solitude of climbing
lichenous rocks. In soft perpetual rain,

cedars aspire to vanishing point in the sky,
then, sea-stained and enormous, niched for foothold,
lichenous rocks, in soft perpetual rain.
Each, agile or clumsy, silently scales them.

Then, see: Stained and enormous, niched for foothold
by tidepools sloshing broken shells and driftwood
(each, agile or clumsy, silently scales them
to her own size), boulders embrace the Sound.

By tidepools sloshing broken shells, and driftwood
from where her moorline loops back loosely
to her own sides (boulders embrace the sound
there) is a serviceable wooden dory.

FROM PROVENCE

At the Régence, I wonder, is the brain
fed by the eye, or does it feed the eye?
On the red tabletop, sunlit, my glass,
half-full, releases fizz into the air.
Two women at the next table look like
Park Slope dykes. Or are they speaking French?

(Some Park Slope dykes speak perfectly good French,
but wouldn't, here.) I do have dykes on the brain.
"I never met a woman I wouldn't like,"
said Natalie Barney, catching the green eye
of the teen-aged Polish painter in an air-
man's casque of matching green lamé. Her glass

of pear-colored pastis crackling on *glace
brisée* (as it was happening in French)
stood precisely between them. The night air
was laced with lavender. I think the brain
informs the genitals of what the eye
suspects. "I'm never certain if I'd like

to do what I think with somebody I like,"
said the girl, who is transforming in the glass
of fiction what I might have said if I
were approached by Natalie Barney, speaking French,
as I'd have to, to say to those women (Brain-
storm for something plausible), "The air

smells of the sea this morning. You've an *air
sympat'*, and though it's bold of me, I'd like
to know you." But habit exiles the brain,
reactionary anarchist, with glass
a foot thick between thought and action. Frenchwomen wear short hair, but not plaid shirts, and eye

makeup is a giveway. Now I
actually *need* a light. With the air
of a habituée, one reads a French
newspaper. The other, who does look like
someone I know, stands up, empties her glass
of orange juice. The young Pole was a Brain

at school. Brains counted but (she squinted) eyes
are seen while seeing, not like one-way glass.
The Frenchwomen have vanished in thin air!

CANZONE

Consider the three functions of the tongue:
taste, speech, the telegraphy of pleasure,
are not confused in any human tongue;
yet, sinewy and singular, the tongue
accomplishes what, perhaps, no other organ
can. Were I to speak of giving tongue,
you'd think two things at least; and a cooked tongue,
sliced, on a plate, with caper sauce, which I give
my guest for lunch, is one more, to which she'd give
the careful concentration of her tongue
twice over, to appreciate the taste
and to express—it would be in good taste—

a gastronomic memory the taste
called to mind, and mind brought back to tongue.
There is a paucity of words for taste:
sweet, sour, bitter, salty. Any taste,
however multiplicitous its pleasure,
complex its execution (I might taste
that sauce ten times in cooking, change its taste
with herbal subtleties, chromatic organ
tones of clove and basil, good with organ
meats) must be described with those few taste-
words, or with metaphors, to give
my version of sensations it would give

a neophyte, deciding whether to give
it a try. She might develop a taste.
(You try things once; I think you have to give
two chances, though, to know your mind, or give
up on novelties.) Your mother tongue
nurtures, has the subtleties which give
flavor to words, and words to flavor, give
the by no means subsidiary pleasure
of being able to describe a pleasure
and recreate it. Making words, we give
the private contemplations of each organ
to the others, and to others, organ-

ize sensations into thoughts. Sentient organ-
isms, we symbolize feeling, give
the spectrum (that's a symbol) each sense organ
perceives, by analogy, to others. Disorgan-
ization of the senses is an acquired taste
we all acquire; as speaking beasts, it's organ-
ic to our discourse. The first organ
of acknowledged communion is the tongue
(tripartite diplomat, which after tongu-
ing a less voluble expressive organ
to wordless efflorescences of pleasure
offers up words to reaffirm the pleasure).

That's a primary difficulty: pleasure
means something, and something different, for each
    organ;
each person, too. I may take exquisite pleasure
in boiled eel, or blancmange—or not. One pleasure
of language is making known what not to give.
And think of a bar of lavender soap, a pleasure
to see and, moistened, rub on your skin, a pleasure
especially to smell, but if you taste
it (though smell is most akin to taste)
what you experience will not be pleasure;
you almost retch, grimace, stick out your tongue,
slosh rinses of ice water over your tongue.

But I would rather think about your tongue
experiencing and transmitting pleasure
to one or another multi-sensual organ
—like memory. Whoever wants to give
only one meaning to that, has untutored taste.

TAKING NOTICE

TAKING NOTICE

"two women together is a work
nothing in civilization has made simple"
    Adrienne Rich: *XXI Love Poems*

1
My child wants dolls, a tutu, that girls' world made
pretty and facile. Sometimes. Sometimes I
want you around uncomplicatedly.
Work every day; love (the same one) every
night: old songs and new choir the parade
of coupled women whose fidelity
is a dyke icon. You are right: if we
came to new love and friendship with a sad
baggage of endings, we would come in bad
faith, and bring, rooted already, seed
of a splitting. Serial monogamy
is a cogwheeled hurt, though you don't like the word.
The neighbor's tireless radio sings lies
through the thin wall behind my desk and bed.

2

Morning: the phone jangles me from words: you,
working at his place, where you slept last night,
missed me. You'll bring drawings. I missed you too.
What centers, palpably swelling my tight
chest: lust, tenderness, an itch of tears.
Three Swedish Ivy rootlings get a pot.
Wash earth-crumbed hands, strip, put long underwear
on, tug, zip, buckle, tie, button, go out—
a mailbox full of bills and circulars.
I trust you: it's a knife-edge of surprise
through words I couldn't write down, subvocalize
across Eighty-First Street, cold as it was
at eight when I put Iva on the bus,
stalling through iced slush between frost-rimed cars.

3

When that jackbooted choreography
sends hobnailed cabrioles across a brain,
the stroked iron pulling lovers together pulls
them apart. Through the ecstatic reverie
of hands, eyes, mouths, our surfaces' silken
sparking, heraldic plants and animals
alive on our tender cartography,
the homesick victim glimpses the coast of pain,
hears the familiar argot of denial.
Woman I love, as old, as new to me
as any moment of delight risked in
my lumpy heretofore unbeautiful
skin, if I lost myself in you I'd be
no better lost than any other woman.

4

She twists scraps of her hair in unshelled snails
crossed by two hairpins. It takes forty-five
minutes. I'm twelve. I've come in to pee. I've
left *Amazing Stories* and *Weird Tales*
in the hamper. "Don't believe what you read.
Women who let men use them are worse than
whores. Men despise them. I can understand
prostitutes, never 'free love.' " Not freed
to tell her what I thought of *More Than Human*,
I wipe between my mottled oversized
girl-haunches. I'll be one of the despised,
I know, as she forbids with her woman's
body, flaccid, gaunt in a greyed nightgown,
something more culpable for us than "men."

5

"I never will be only a Lesbian."
Bare rubber, wedged beside its tube of cream
in the bookshelf near your bed, your diaphragm
lies on Jane Cooper's poem and Gertrude Stein.
I've torn our warm cocoon again. I listen.
Our sweatered breasts nuzzle under the quilt.
(Yes, there's one in my bathroom cabinet;
unused, now.) If a man sleeps with men, and women,
he's *queer: vide* Wilde, Goodman, Gide, Verlaine.
A woman who does can be "passionately
heterosexual" (said Norman Pearson of H. D.).
Anyone's love with women doesn't count.
Rhetoric, this. You talk about your friend.
I hold you, wanting whatever I want.

6

Angry, I speak, and pass the hurt to you,
your pencil-smudged face naked like a child's.
Each time we don't know what we're getting into
or out of. Later, washed out and reconciled,
we wait on the subway platform, Mutt and Jeff
puffed out with football socks and Duofolds,
word-shy, habitually bold enough
to sit thigh against corduroy thigh and hold
hands; though, ungendered in thick winter gear,
only your cheeks' epicene ivory
makes us the same sex. No one looks healthy
in the perpetual fluorescence. Here
(you say) the light is the same night and day,
but it feels like night at night anyway.

7

If we talk, we're too tired to make love; if we
make love, these days, there's hardly time to talk.
We sit to share supper once, twice a week.
You're red and white with cold; we're brusque, scared,
    shy.
Difficult speech curdles the café au lait
next morning. In the short twelve hours between
we rubbed, laughed, tongued, exhorted, listened, came,
slept like packed spoons. Wrapped up against the day
we trudge through slush as far as the downtown
subway, brush cold-tattered lips. You're gone
to hunch sock-shod over your camera, while
I stare a spiral notebook down six miles
north, indulging some rich weave of weeks where
we'd work, play, not cross-reference calendars.

8

The sitter, sniffling, leaves, clicks the door shut.
Shuck boots; back from Womanbooks. Iva fights
the quilt in her top bunk, in striped underwear.
A painter read from six months journals, through
learning she loved a woman, at forty-two.
If you were here, we'd compare pasts, compare
process to language, art; you're not, tonight.
Back at the revolution all is not
well. We, women, patient mockers of our own
enterprise, are mined with self-destruction.
We build what we need. We wreck what we build.
I'm making coffee when the telephone
rings: you, ducked into a booth across town?
Another woman, friend, as risked, as real.

9

In my boots and blazer I feel like Julien Sorel.
Should I bow from the waist, flourish my hand
three rolls from crown to knee? No, I'm polite and
verbose. Films; drinks; the meeting goes as well
as it could, until five o'clock when he
leaves, and I wax vehement over beer
bottles. Look, baby, I *want* to be queer,
it's the light at the other end of the
long march, et cetera. Cut: a streamlined
she-torso with no feet, no hands, no head;
intercut penis/hammer; eye reads: blows:
his filmed image of—you? Woman? Who knows
(I don't) what's between you two. We spar down
slicked streets to your stop; kiss. I walk downtown.

10

The grizzled doorman lets the doctors' wives
into and out of the rainstorm. Thirty-year-
old mothers hive here till their men's careers
regroup the swarm for boxed suburban lives.
The doorman's sixty, football-shouldered, white.
The multi-racial anoraked interns
will earn, per year, at forty, more than he earns
in ten. Maybe one-tenth of the scrubbed bright
wives will earn his wages; fewer do.
Knees dovetailed at The Duchess, I'm giving you
my hours with a talk-starved woman I knew there
through her tough small girl, while on the polished
    square
at our boot-toes blue-jeaned women slow-dance
to a rhythmic alto plaint of ruined romance.

11

In the Public Theater lobby, I wait for Marie.
Black overcoat, brown plait: two people waltz
close, through the crowd's buzz. I watch, finding fault
with the dance's hierarchic He and She.
They weave past; Tall leads, Short follows. I see
they're women. I love them. I stand near
them, grin, wish I wore a lavender star.
Marie's here, blinking, owlish. We hug. We
go upstairs. The two women sit one row
ahead, kissing. I look at them, look away.
They are more edifying than the play
(will they laugh at woman-made misogyny?
Yes . . .) but I shouldn't stare, and when I do
I flush above the belt and throb below.

12

You're high on work, bouncing words off the ceiling
as we lie down, go down into a flurry of down,
arms and legs enlaced. My tongue around
your hillocks shudders your pleasure, feeling
its own rough touch call the blood-rush swelling
everything mutable to immanence.
We giggle at our fork-tongued eloquence,
gasp at our fingers' dazzling slide. You're telling
me about Wittgenstein and Gertrude Stein
images juxtaposed on a white wall
moving, the metaphysics of a meal
we shared, till we kiss ourselves to a wine-
drenched feast whose mute wit is a mutual
silence honed in our rapt mouths to a sign.

13

No better lost than any other woman
turned resolutely from the common pool
of our erased, emended history,
I think of water, in this book-strewn room. In
another room, my daughter, home from school,
audibly murmurs "spanking, stupid, angry
voice"—a closet drama where I am
played second-hand to unresisting doll
daughters. Mother and daughter both, I see
myself, the furious and unforgiven;
myself, the terrified and terrible;
the child punished into autonomy;
the unhealed woman hearing her own voice damn
her to the nightmares of the brooding girl.

14

And I shout at Iva, whine at you. Easily
we choose up for nuclear family,
with me the indirect, snivelling, put-upon
mother/wife, child's villain, feminist heroine,
bore. On thick white plates the failed communion
congeals. Iva bawls in her room. You're on
edge, worked out, fed up, could leave. Shakily
we stop. You wash dishes, drop one; it breaks. We
should laugh. We don't. A potted plant crashed too.
Frowning, I salvage the crushed shoots, while you
deflect my scowl with yours. You leave a phone
message for your friend, while I read one
last picture book, permit a bedtime drink
to a nude child, who's forgiven me—I think.

15

Through wet August nights we were the revolution crawling forward on each other's
bellies. Our anecdotes about our mothers
told what would be foible, what unforgiv-
able. Twenty-seven, thirty-six, five,
we three amble, howl at the March full moon
over housing projects. Iva hangs on
our elbows. "Drag me!" Our tensed arms heft live
weight, grubby and kicking. Your tired pale
face shifts in the moon-pool: a farm woman,
a raw boy, a red-lipped hedonist.
Night slims down, warms up toward our third season.
I lean above my unkempt child toward all
of them. She tugs us, "I *hate* to be kissed!"

16

Dreams play diverse cadenzas of betrayal.
I wake word-foundered. Anything I say
discovers discord. Chin to squared-off chin,
crossed arms, I worry you, "How do you feel?"
"Anxious. I feel cut off and far away."
You and I have done, will do this again:
one querulous; response: one inflexible.
I A-train uptown through the ordinary
assaults. MEN STONE FEM LIBBERS IN IRAN.
Childless, anonymous, accountable,
I gauge how wide apart to stake my knees.
Most of the faces facing me are brown.
None of the choices facing me are simple.
I can't, today, begin a sentence "We . . ."

17

I hold you, wanting whatever I want:
to taste cold water; to get up and pee;
to fuck; to know there might be space named "we"
to build on. I tend to the first two, can't
have all. You're asleep. Still in underpants,
I wash the percolator out, start coffee,
write, cross out, write more. Anxiety
shifts through the placed words' patterns, takes
      distance
enough that when you say my name, I lie
with you, loosened, in your waking fragrance:
soaped hair, warm bread of your skin, exhaled mint.
My eyes encounter your lacustrine eyes,
where you might, I might, miscall lust, clarity,
and I hook my tongue on something like a sentence.

18

I'll tell you what I don't want: an affair:
love, by appointment only, twice a week;
grimy, gratuitous life lived elsewhere
with others. When it's easier to speak
about than to you, when I think of you
more than I'm with you, more anxious than tender,
I feel less than a friend. There's work to do.
Artist, woman, I love you; craft and gender,
if we're antagonists, aren't in dispute.
Love starts with circumstance; it grows with care
to something self-sufficient, centered, root
from which the cultivators branch, the air
renewing them transpired rich from its pores.
Or so I hoped while I was celibate.

19

When I read poems to the art students
I wanted you there; when my ephebes, shar-
ing craft I taught, showed off, I wanted you there;
when I talk a woman around imprudence,
when I orchestrate a meeting or a meal,
when my thoughts unroll imaginal sentences,
when I come through better than I thought I was,
I want you there. But I surface seasick, feel
desire and apprehension lashed like stones
to me. Reeled toward you in the elevator,
I shrink inches from my accomplished stature
of thoughtful hero, whom you haven't seen,
diminishing to needy lover, green
with doubt and necessarily alone.

20

You separate perception from perceiver;
I make it sound like virtue that I can't.
In this imaginary argument
we've had repeatedly when we're together,
my mind is limbic, weighted like the weather.
You're sunlit on another continent.
It's rained five days here. The first two I spent
indoors, ate cheese, read magazines, neither
nourished nor informed. My anger paired
with your absence: lonely parameters.
I want to be the child-philosopher
cross-legged in the drop-leaf table's shelter;
bare legs crossed on the nubbly pile, who felt her
mind's flux find form in fixed faces of chairs.

21

Down from the hills at dawn, a thunderstorm
pounded the cabin roof. Indoors, I rolled
to the wall, a log quilted against spring cold,
and wove the noise into a ravelling dream
whose threads snapped into syllables Marie
was muttering from the upper bunk in clear
incoherence. You're not here. Iva's not here.
We sat on the porch late, in luxury
of rambling childless conversation, ate
a steak cooked on the camp stove, with Bordeaux
from New Paltz, talked more, turned in. Candlelit
again, impatient and disconsolate,
I wait afternoon rains out, rummage through
scrap thoughts while Marie writes, stalled, missing you.

22

The late-May weather's risky as a mood.
Yesterday's freighted clouds have burned away
leaving scoured sky, mud, sunlight, solitude
I frame in tin cups of thermos coffee
back on the porch with Marie. Heliotrope,
I lodge, knees up in weeds, on a gravelled slope
where tall white pines light candles for the summer.
On my knapsack strap, a V-winged bomber
modelled from a scarab perches on moon-
jitney legs, a horsefly numbed with noon
sun. I've learned to pick out a late wood-
thrush song enlacing the percussive jays.
This respite from inclement weather could
(clouds are banking up, though) last through the day.

23

As yoked to her by absence as by presence,
I image, fifteen minutes since she's gone,
her sneakers pushing leaves up as she ran
into the woods, urged on to independence
by me. Feet on the porch rail, I drink silence,
thinking: She has to cross the road alone.
If she doesn't find anyone at home
—the six-year-old gone shopping with his parents—
will she get panicky and lose her way?
Revenant, you nap. Marie drove to town.
I look up from my book, identify
the she-cardinal's sanguine rose-brown,
then check my watch. From down the path comes "Hey,
Mom!" Forty-five minutes on my own.

24
Strata of August 12: portable typewriter,
seashell ashtray, blue-and-white plastic lighter,
a jagged ochre flint from the Val d'Oise,
two amber quartz flakes, two packs of Gauloises,
tan spiral notebook, brown spiral address
book, a friend's typed essay on loneliness,
her card from Russian River, a map of France,
a blank postcard of market day in Vence,
four letters in four colored envelopes,
typing pad, cold coffee in a glass cup,
airmail envelopes in a paper band,
two felt pens, one capped, one in a beige hand,
writing, straw mat, glossy black paint that pulls
the eye on reflected light to the facing hills.

25
We work, play, don't cross-reference calendars
here. Sun gilds a scrub-oak hill; the fig tree
drops purple dry first fruit on the cement
terrace that's, for the rest of August, ours,
where you project perspectives, blond head bent
to big papers. I chart stratigraphy
of my desk, glimpse, in a pitcher, flowers
you brought, for our year, though we're both diffident
to celebrate. I start letters, can't write
what it's like, face to face, learning to live
through four A.M. eruptions, when we fight
like bruised children we were. Can I believe
persistent love demands change, not forgive-
ness, accept the hard gift of your different sight?

A NOTE ABOUT THE AUTHOR

Marilyn Hacker is the author of two other books of poetry: *Separations* and *Presentation Piece*, which was a Lamont Poetry Selection of the Academy of American Poets and received the National Book Award for Poetry in 1975. She was born in New York City and lives there now, after a decade in San Francisco and London, with her daughter Iva, aged six. She is the recipient of a Creative Artists Public Service Grant and of a Guggenheim Fellowship for 1980.

A NOTE ON THE TYPE

The text of this book was set on the Linotype in Palatino, a type face designed by the noted German typographer Hermann Zapf. Named after Giovanbattista Palatino, a writing master of Renaissance Italy, Palatino was the first of Zapf's type faces to be introduced to America. The first designs for the face were made in 1948, and the fonts for the complete face were issued between 1950 and 1952. Like all Zapf-designed type faces, Palatino is beautifully balanced and exceedingly readable.

Composed by Maryland Linotype Composition Co., Inc. Baltimore, Maryland. Printed and bound by The Haddon Craftsmen, Scranton, Pennsylvania.

Typography and binding design by Anne J. Pentola, based on a design by Camilla Filancia